WHAT PECAN LIGHT

WHAT PECAN LIGHT

POEMS

HAN VANDERHART

BULL★CITY
PRESS
DURHAM, NORTH CAROLINA

What Pecan Light

Library of Congress Cataloging-in-Publication Data

Names: VanderHart, Han, 1985- author.
Title: What pecan light : poems / Han VanderHart.
Description: Durham, North Carolina : Bull City Press, [2022] | Includes bibliographical references.
Identifiers: LCCN 2022935041 (print) | LCCN 2021000967 (ebook) | ISBN 9781949344356 (paperback) | ISBN 9781949344271 (ebook)
Subjects: LCSH: Southern States--Poetry. | LCGFT: Poetry.
Classification: LCC PS3622.A59245 W48 2021 (print) | LCC PS3622.A59245 (ebook) | DDC 811/.6--dc23
LC record available at https://lccn.loc.gov/2022935041
LC ebook record available at https://lccn.loc.gov/2021000967

second edition

Published in the United States of America
Book design by Spock and Associates with Savannah Bradley

Cover artwork: *Joined* by Rachael DiRenna

Published by BULL CITY PRESS
1217 Odyssey Drive
Durham, NC 27713
www.BullCityPress.com

CONTENTS

What Escaped   3

"Western One of Top Parish Broiler Producers" (*Ruston Leader*, 1960)   5

High Cotton   6

Chicken Farming in the Pelican State   7

Tractors   8

Chicken Coop   10

Song of the South   11

Having Taken Part in the Late Rebellion   12

The Lives of My Childhood   13

Confederate Monuments   14

Poem Ending in a Line from C.D. Wright   15

Diving Into the Wreck   17

Post-Antebellum in the States   18

Dixie Land Delight   20

Post-Katrina   21

Unwashed   22

Homily on the Hand and Eye   23

This Hour   24

The Confederate Flag Is a War Flag   26

To the Flaggers, Erecting Confederate Flags in the Commonwealth
of Virginia   28

From the Nests of Buff Orpingtons, Rhode Island Reds, and Barred Rocks   29

When we are not talking about race in the South we are talking about race
in the South   30

History As a Bottle Tree   31

Locusts or Complaint As Protest   32

Confederate Statues Are Falling This Morning   33

On the Anniversary of the Mass Shooting at Virginia Tech (2007) 35

Poem Beginning with a Line from Claudia Rankine 36

Remembering That My Grandfather Hunted Men with Dogs in the

       Alabama Woods 37

Why She Wears Hummingbirds on Fishing Line around Her Neck 38

Regarding the Hooding of the Daughters of the Confederacy Monument 39

A Visitor Says Things Are Rotting in Durham, North Carolina 40

Where Art Thou: A Family Account 41

Of Fences and Surrender 44

In a Dream I Am at a Poetry Reading and I Look Out the Window 46

When Someone Says a Poem Is Masterful 47

It Was a Field before It Was a Battlefield 49

The Supper Book 50

Confession 51

Night Is the Time of Monument Removal 52

The Light Has Always Been Going Down 53

This Is the Barbecue We Had Last Night 55

Notes 57

Acknowledgments 59

About the Author 61

I don't expect the light
to save me, but I do believe
in the ritual.

Linda Gregg

Not the pigs. Not the seventeen roosters
from the spring incubators. Not the hens

taken by farmyard parasites, fed on
electrolytes. Not the bantam, taken by

hawk. Little bird, feathers on its feet.
Not the eight African Grey geese, spread

like cotton pieces on the lawn after
the Jack Russells, who did escape.

What do we farm but loss, and isn't
this also an argument for denying

everything loved? Your brothers
and sisters. Your parents. Better not

keep what you know will not escape
sorrow but will escape you, leave you

looking at a yard of white flowers:
fringed phacelia, appearing as a mist

in spring.

Lots of folks in the area are missing a real bet when they are not taking advantage
of the natural fertilizer from chicken droppings. A person can get free fertilizer for
raising the chickens and then get paid for mediately!

— A. L. Hethcox

These are the words I have
from my grandfather—his wisdom on how
a person can get free from spending more
than they need to, running a farm. How a person
can work with and not against the ground
piling up beneath the chickens, squat
in their boxed rows. What does it mean
for a person to miss *a real bet*? A deal you
can count on, steady as droppings
on a commercial chicken farm. "Get paid for
mediately!" he says, and means *reuse* and
be resourceful. My father says my grandfather
hired both black and white farm laborers.
What do I do with this knowledge? Louisiana is
a land fertilized with segregation, the soil and water
heavy with it. I'm told that once a year,
my grandfather would haul a load of chicken
manure, spread it on his suburban lawn.
My mother says that the neighbors complained
each time. My father says that when it rained
the smell was putrefying.

I never saw it. Only corn at ankle, knee,
then shoulder height. The low soy fields.
The sorghum twisting like green ribbons.
We were children, running through,
stumbling over dirt clods. You can't run
through a newly disced field, or you shouldn't.
Remember pulling a shoot of sorghum?
The pale green stem, sugar bead at its end.
The silos filled with it, like the parable of
the wealthy farmer. The harvest rolled in.

Still, the white fields patched the counties
'round my family's poultry farm. You wear
a mask on farms so the dust doesn't fill
your airways. Did my father leave his off?
My brother, one summer on a turkey farm, did.
Spent the fall coughing out an infection. Knew
what had caused it. Knew what ailed him.
Left the mask off anyway. Breathed in.

It's not like we can choose what spears us through the heart.
What lone cedar strikes us as the clouds burn off at noon.
What pecan light. What clue as to how a person lives
or dies—clew like the ball of yarn at the heart of the
maze. Follow and you will escape the bull-headed man.
My father's father owned the second-largest chicken
farm in the state of Louisiana. A million layers, three million
broilers, sacrificed every three months. My father's father
had a heart attack at the Sunday breakfast table, eggs on the
plate before him. My uncle upstairs. My father enlisted
in the army. Three months earlier, he underwent triple
bypass surgery. Three years earlier, he sold the lion's share
of his farm to a leopard salesman with good business
sense. My father said it broke his heart. I never expected
a sentimental explanation, but nicknames for the state
of Louisiana include *Sugar State* and *Sportsman's*
Paradise, Child of the Mississippi. My father said
when he was a child, his father always left a fried egg
and half a slice of toast on his plate, for my father to eat.

We never owned one. A tractor
was something you borrowed

from a neighbor whose soy
was already leafing the field.

My mother started us young
in the garden, with a hoe taller

than our heads, its wooden handle
knocking our ears. My life started

as a good weeding, early
in the morning, dew still

on the beans and spider webs.
There was a mist sometimes

like a cotton sea. I remember
driving home from college,

rounding the bend on 95, seeing
the John Deere tractors greening

the hill above traffic—it lifted
my heart every time to see them.

In *Old Farm, New Farm*, a children's
book, the farm starts as a thing

more full of holes than not. Puddles
spotting the farmyard, the tractor's

seat missing. The harrow's teeth
gone to rust. The farmer milks

the cows first, mends the fences.
Repairs the greenhouse panes of glass.

Knows he can leave the tractor 'til
spring, and knows he can't live

without it. The end of the book
is pots of jam and cream.

It's nothing more than a wooden box
on stilts. A slanted roof against snow and rain.

At first it's nothing more than space. A plot
of ground. And then a frame like a rib

bone followed by another rib, and another.
It's what my mother always wanted.

Not low and low-roofed, so the gatherer must
stoop. But high. Unfloodable. Unfoxable.

The hawks could only gaze, desiring,
through the chicken wire. The black snakes

entered my father's shed instead, fried
themselves in black loops on the electrics.

I posed there, in the coop's frame, halfway
built. Someone took my picture, my face

turned in profile to the fields, the sedge
grass growing copper and sweet.

See the yellow mustard flowers in my hand,
against my blue denim dress. Oh coop.

You were what my mother had always
wanted. She sighed when we moved.

Is sweet potato pie. Is seed potatoes,
quartered and dropped in the furrows
in the spring. Is potatoes and pork loin
gravy. Always gravy. A cast iron skillet.
Eggs and biscuits in the morning.
Methodism. The humidity of our hearts.
Church on Sunday morning. A pew
expected, set aside for the family.
Picking beans. Not drinking. Not
acknowledging porn. Getting married.
Not talking about divorce. The step
sister who married and lives in Alaska.
No one chooses their family. Most of
all, the song is black and white. Most of all
we don't talk about it. We don't even hum.
The biscuits, steaming, the apple butter
brown and velvet in its half-pint jars.
We name the pigs Caesar and Pompeii
knowing neither of them will survive.

John "Jack" Allums (1810–1870)

My third-great-grandfather on my mother's mother's side enslaved.

Lost the largest part of his "property" to the Emancipation Proclamation.

His script or his lawyer's confesses as much in his Confederate Application
      for Pardon.

Sent to the Department of Justice.

Sent to His Excellency Andrew Johnson, President of the United States.

He wanted his property back—the land part. Probably the person part, too, but
      Johnson forbade it.

It says so in the pardon Johnson gave my third-great-grandfather, Jack Allums, third
      lieutenant in the Macon County Reserves. The Home Guard. Howell
      Peebles' Company.

He was 54 or 58.

By his account, Allums did not order the taking of Fort Morgan or Mount Vernon
      Arsenal, nor aid in nor advise the taking of either of them.

Did not serve on any Vigilance Committee during the war.

Did not shoot or hang any person nor aid in shooting or hanging anyone for real or
      supposed disloyalty to the Confederate States.

He writes this twice.

He did not order or engage in hunting anyone with dogs who was disloyal, or
      supposed to be disloyal to the Confederate States.

He was opposed to Cessession [sic], until the ordinance passed Jan. 11, 1861, and then
      he supported the action of his state, Alabama.

He has suffered greatly by depredations during the existence of hostilities. He has
      not accumulated property during the Rebellion.

He will endeavor to be a peaceful and loyal citizen in the future.

Enslaved persons, but for this he does not ask pardon.

are paper dolls from a book of *Civil War*
Southern Belles, in sea-green brocade

ball gowns. Looped hair and leg-of-mutton
sleeves. Pantaloons like walking clouds.

They went with men in gray uniforms
and swords to dance. I made them go.

The gowns slipped over their white and pink
chemises. The corseted stays. My scissors

were Patience herself, cutting the gowns.
The hat with peacock feathers. The tiny fan.

After the ball I took off their clothes.
The bonnets with flowers and ribbons.

I folded back the tabs of their long
nightgowns over their paper bodies.

The lace nightcaps. Under the gown
hems were pairs of satin slippers.

I did not even need to look. The souls
of the paper dolls counted on that—

slept in their paper folder as I slept.

Never neutral, [monuments] tend to represent the narratives and memories of those citizens with the political power and money to construct them.

— Natasha Trethewey

Of equestrian statues it is said
both equine legs in the air: the rider
died in battle, one leg in the air: dead
by wounds inflicted in battle, legs
on the ground: survived the battle.

But the rubric is folklore to keep
us looking longer at the legs
of horse and rider, to keep us there.

Whereas symbols of the Southern army
include holidays and the names
of schools, roads, parks, bridges,
counties, cities, lakes, dams, military
bases, and other public works.

Such that our children will both know
and not know the Confederacy.

POEM ENDING IN A LINE FROM C.D. WRIGHT

For the front yard mimosa pinking its boughs
above the old truck | and the congregationalist urge

to give account before witnesses | I write
and talk | at the park | telling my neighbor

how a rebel war flag flies over Interstate 95
and he says | *It's hard—people had family die*

in that war | and he doesn't mean Iraq | or drones
or the border our neighbors' children die to cross | no

he means the Civil War | but whose uncle or brother
died at Appomattox? | No one in my family

remembers | I had to do the work of books
to find what I did not want to find | history

with its long oppressive arm | its roll calls
and musters | enlistment dates | pension records

Confederate Applications for Pardon | Isn't
it enough | my fathers and uncles | my brothers

aunts | grandmother and grandfathers
sprang from the South and have done the work

of war? | It is not enough | my mouth is small
a little bole on a live oak | but when my neighbor

says *who died* | doesn't he mean who is dying?
And when he nods, says *oh yeah, people bitching*

about the flag | I recollect the poet who said
to be ashamed is to be American

Beren, five years, asks to cuddle. I lift up my arm like a wing in response. I'm reading a reprint of *Diving Into the Wreck*. The words stream black in the air. We talk about the scuba diver's mask—it pumps our blood with power. His head leans in. He is content to listen, adrift in the plankton bloom of sound. His fingers stroke my hand as Rich pulls her reader, rung by rung, into the opaque ocean. Crenelated beings swim and dodge around us. I wonder if my fellow diver sees the sunken ship. *The ribs of the disaster. This is the place.* The poem ends. *What is a myth?* I ask. *It is—something like a legend*, he says. His examples of myth are awake with dragons. Every morning, he is a new kind of dragon.

His dragons are different than mine—they have no fields of violence.

We try not to mention history
at the Winn-Dixie—

or in Bay Saint Louis, lifting
the houses back after Katrina.

I built a house with you there,
spackled the walls. The flood lines

waving above us. The sticky
whiteness of spackle. Marry me.

As a child I ran with a rebel flag
and we did not question

our play, which was violent
and harmonized with our idea of God.

We asked: if you could be blue
or gray, what would you be?

Gray, always gray. We lay
on the wall in Devil's Den, imitated

the dead boy soldier. A rebel
sharpshooter, CSC on his buckle.

His body moved, posed in death—
theater so real we perform it again.

We try not to mention it, but we copy
war with panes of glass, wet negatives.

Collodion: a viscous solution
applied to both wounds and films.

✍

I was born in Virginia, a state whose
wealth came from plantations.

Moved house, birthed my first child
in Maryland, another plantation state.

Moved again, birthed my second child
in North Carolina, a third plantation state.

Daddy is from Little Rock,
Arkansas. Mama met Daddy

in Louisiana. On my LSU class
ring, handed to me: a pelican,

feeding its young from its breast.
Spilling its blood in compassion.

So like Christ. So unlike Louisiana,
Arkansas, the Carolinas, Virginia.

✍

We don't mention it, but we
kept the Confederate colors,

pressed them into stars and bars.

Isn't the truck parked in the holler.
Is the black walnuts, rolling down
in autumn, pungent green husks
blackening as the walnuts swell
inside. Our Mennonite neighbors
paid their children ten cents for a
#10 can, filled with shelled fruit.
We took our hammers to them.
We broke them open and found
the meat. We had so little time
for trouble, when I was young,
when the walnuts rolled in, or
the apples, or tomatoes. Boiling
or paring or peeling. Slaughtering
the chickens and hogs, the grinder
turning, the scrapple boiling in the pot.
I've looked in the glassy eyes of dead
things. I've washed feathers and blood
from my hands. I've laid down on
a quilt, on an August day, watched
the threads slip from their seams.

Bay St. Louis, Mississippi

We went in the spring. The magnolias blooming, flowers large as dinner plates. The bay bridge, new. The demolition team wrestled fridges that had sat for a year in the heat to the curbs. We called what spilled from them when they tipped and the duct tape gave *fridge juice*. It spilled on my brother. Before the fridge removals, everyone wanted to demolish. Swing a hammer at flooded walls. You were moved to my building team for want of builders. We fell in love with spackle on our hands, in our hair. Remember the night of the crab feast? *Come and pick*, they said. We rolled in, end of the work week. By the house with the tables full of crabs: an uncleared lot. *Clear it before dinner*, we were told. Our youth director threw his hat. We became happy workers: cleared the brush and trees and trash. After that, sweat dripping, tables of hot crab on brown paper. You went to it. I went to the van, sat in the semi-cool, ate a hot dog. Southern heart longing for AC, a dry sofa, a Coke. The donated food we ate that week—turkey jerky and PB&J—molded in the humidity. Softened and disappeared like drywall in the houses you could put a hand through. One woman who used to own a home drove to Walmart and fed us when she heard. Joy is a yogurt and bologna on fresh white bread. We had not seen love before like that, among the FEMA trailers. To not grow weary. To build to code.

My mother sends me unwashed eggs.
I have forgotten what streaks an egg.

The blood and shit of laying, even in straw.
How hands must wash each egg. How

unwashed eggs travel best, keep best;
eggs laid as the hen and God intended.

It's not only chickens that arrive this way.
We are washed. We forget arriving covered

in our mother's blood and vernix, sometimes
our own meconium, a prenatal term for shit.

My second child came five days early.
He had vernix like a cream around him.

He smelled like butter, like a bakery.
I didn't want to wash him. Not yet.

That learned
    to catch a chicken
        running, wheeling

headless in the yard,
    escaped from my brother's
        butchering hand.

That caught its feet
    and held on until
        the wings stopped flapping.

That dipped it into
    boiling water, hung
        its feet on the fence.

That plucked the wet
    feathers, down
        to the pinfeathers

and the yellow bud of fat
    below each, to the skin
        dimpled and bare.

The lesson of the broiler
    chicken is that we are bare.
        Under feathers, we are all bare.

this is the breakfast hour
this is the writing hour

this is the dew hour
the wild mustard beside

the railway tracks hour
the hour of loss for mothers

for any kind of kin shot
yesterday in the park

this is the yellow-green hour
the lauds-after-matins hour

the hour of the doe and her
two fawns crossing the tracks,

the hour of nosing forward
with our heads down scenting

for food, for danger, for grace
near the wild mustard and the tracks

this is the hour I make coffee
alone and miss the child-noise

of your breakfast, your loud
spoon smacking the tabletop

this is the hour our neighbor
will not see her son again

this is the hour before her next
hour, before the next hour and

the hour after that, this is
a grief-table of hours for her

skidding its wooden surface
out before her like narrow tracks

this is the hour of doe and fawns,
of milk for four, five months

It soars from the bed of
a pickup truck, roaring

through town, the bars of Dixie
blaring out the window.

This was last summer in Durham,
North Carolina—a *blue city*.

Last night, my son cried
beside me when we read

about the Birmingham
bombing, 1963:

Addie Mae Collins, Carole Robertson,
Cynthia Wesley, Carol Denise McNair—

killed in their Sunday School
dresses, at church.

Later that day, Johnny Robinson
and friends threw rocks at a car

hung with the rebel flag. The cops
inside the car threw slurs,

glass bottles, bullets—and white
Birmingham killed another boy.

If you cannot cry, ask
what is wrong with your body:

the flag flies in white, Southern
hearts all the long day.

I write this for my mother,
because we are Southern,

and we repeat history,
play it like a reel.

I cannot keep this from my child:
he cries, asks if we can pray.

Mother, hear me: the heart
is muscle and sore.

TO THE FLAGGERS, ERECTING CONFEDERATE FLAGS
IN THE COMMONWEALTH OF VIRGINIA

the heart is muscle and sore

when I consider the burnings—

whose car, whose body got

draped in this Southern cross,

who wears it on their caps

and black T-shirts, who sits

outside their garage by the side

of the road, under this flag

like it is shade—do you recall

what happened to Jonah's

shade, the shade he took

delight in?—a worm in the night

my love, a worm put its mouth

to Jonah's shade and soon

Jonah burned in the light

I remember the double,
sometimes triple
yolks;

the egg laid
in the straw
of a nesting box

without a shell,
soft in its membrane
and my palm;

the day my sister
mixed a cake:
cracked

an egg into the
bowl, over
the sugar and flour,

and the egg had
been sat on by
some longing hen,

overlooked by
gatherers, in the dark
barn corner,

and a chick fell out
the shell, fell
in the bowl—

a partial thing.

And by this, I mean my blue-eyed parents.
Being raised among the guinea fowl and chickens.

And there, you see what I did—who grew up
up in the dust of birds, what generation?

It was all of them: the grandparents I knew
and the ones I did not know, my parents

and my siblings—all of us have watched a hen
shimmy in her dustbowl bath at one time

or another. The breeds change—Leghorns,
Barred and Plymouth Rocks—but the acts

remain the same: the care and the not
caring. The drawing of hot water in winter,

knocking the ice from the frozen pan.
The deworming in April. What we have done

and do for chickens as their minor generations
roll out each spring: damp from the incubators,

the glass misted with moisture and the breath
of the least of these, exhausted in its shell.

HISTORY AS A BOTTLE TREE

Returns us to the enslaved
in the South, placing a bottle

on each broken myrtle branch.
At night, a spirit would catch

in the bottle, like a fruit fly
in a vinegar jar, not able

to wind its way out
the slender mouth, and this

is how evil would be
captured in the South:

visibly, in cobalt blue
or clear glass.

Now empty whiskey
bottles, pop bottles grow

from the arms of trees,
wave in the air.

In their hollows, we keep
our evil spirits.

The cicadas are so loud and large
tonight I call them locusts, hear them

through the windows as they sing
a cadence to evening. One flew

in front of me today and I thought
it a bird—but so loud a *whirr* no bird

could own it. This was after class.
I read my students a poem and they dropped

so silent, it was as if all the locusts
had been eaten in the world. Or

crept underground. Gone quiet.
Gone nymph. Retreated from men,

which is not a word locusts use
for mankind or otherwise. Their notes

have shapes. I hear the points and
angles. They stick to the pines.

What are we for but to make a terrible
noise? To beat our wings before silence.

yesterday my mother and I yelled at each other
      rebel yell   yankee yell

but like the Louisiana earth we are, later
we apologize for saying *fucking*,

for the form, not for the thing itself—
for the wreck, not the cause—

for the breaking of decorum—
for letting the bars on our suburban windows show—

for not quietly eating the crawfish po'boy
with the pink fantail still in it—

for not swimming unmurmuring in the lake
the neighbors all know is polluted.

I have a happy picture of myself
at my grandmother's house in Ruston,

Louisiana: holding a turtle from the lake
with both hands, my hair French braided

by a sister or my mother, not by
the grandmother, rumored

to have been a beauty queen,
now with old corn silk hair and bars

on her windows, not even as exciting
as an ice cream truck trilling its tinny swan lake,

or her green, shag-carpeted floors;
like the turtle in the lake I was willing

to love a polluted thing, to swim and not care—
but the copper pant legs of Confederate men

fold and fall this morning, like so many crimped
hairs on a beauty queen's head, in this humidity.

You were down the road in a barn, a week
and a day after Easter, when it began. When a boy
who could have sat in my poetry class opened
fire, kept firing until thirty-two fell, departed.
You had to be like Dad and Grandad—gold
motes of barn dust drifting like an AgSci
halo around your face, filling your lungs.
Rubber gloves pulled up to your shoulder, a hand
on her hip bone, you artificially inseminate
a cow—life by course assignment—and the calf
still gets called *life*, while of the bodies on campus
we do not say *killed* but *tragedy*. But brother, you
were the kindest killer of chickens. Sharpened the
dull ax. Complained it was not an electric knife.

Mostly I resist the flooding—
except for Tuesday, when it crept
up my shoulder and neck. The doctor
prescribed Valium and prednisone.
My sister drove me. It is worse now
than prelims and a baby propped
on my pillowing abs. It's exhausting
to get up in the morning, to rise,
as it is to lie down at night.
Only the trees, the grass, are not
tired. I have seen the cockroaches,
dropping from the sides of the house.
Landing on their backs, or dragging
a bent leg behind them. In feeling
pity for the roach, I have become
ultimately tired. The least of these
is tired and it is only July. Doesn't
the cockroach inherit the earth.
When will the poor. It is July
and our barbed legs are slipping
on the weathered paneling. In
September the roach will try
again, this time scale the house.

REMEMBERING THAT MY GRANDFATHER
HUNTED MEN WITH DOGS IN THE ALABAMA WOODS

I wonder at the getting of the dogs from the stables, the dog pens.
The pack of hounds needed for the chase. (When I was five or six
my parents had a pair of Bluetick Coonhounds: Roger and Rufus—
those hounds broke into the neighbor's chicken house, caused trouble
where there was none; hounds will find prey for their drive.)
I wonder at my grandfather running, or on a horse, holding a lantern.
That he could hunt men, calling them deserters of the Confederacy,
both aloud and in his thoughts. I wonder at his reasoning, how reason
twists to accommodate the excusing mind; how reason runs
as fast as the dogs when they catch scent, baying in excitement.
The terror of the man discovered, crouched or running in the woods.
If my grandfather used words to justify what came next.
Some acts a person should not imagine. Should fight off, with fists.

after Deborah Luster's Rosesucker Retablo, *1993*

Because her face is haunted,
and causes go so far back here
they scarcely bear the illusion or name
of cause, material or formal. Rather,
the birds are effects of living out of death:
mushrooms lifting from mycelium
rings, invisible under the forest floor.
Spores drifting in the air. A burr
in an animal's coat. Her mouth
tired like a fox's fur when mange
takes over and it sheds but doesn't
reveal a new fox. Maybe the birds
keep away snakes, like a snake
hung in a tree keeps away drought
by bringing on rain. Maybe cause
and effect are dirt and sky and little
else beyond. Here is the rain. It comes
like a child, listening to no one
but its own internal vane of weather.

REGARDING THE HOODING OF
THE DAUGHTERS OF THE CONFEDERACY MONUMENT

Raleigh, North Carolina

Riot in the magnolias   at the thought
purple and white clamshell blossoms   quaking—

The Daughters of the Confederacy   caught
in the white corners of pillowcases   Monday morning:

The statue: mother holding child   tenderly
as one holds in secret   a feeling   the banner over them

Not love   but what ordinary people   thought
could be buried   and what has risen   zombie-like

No   what was always there   like the magnolias
our eyes pulled to all that   spun glory   that demand for white

Attention   a resurrection   on repeat
like the magnolias blooming   again   this week

A VISITOR SAYS THINGS ARE ROTTING IN DURHAM, NORTH CAROLINA

We are mostly the humidity. Our politics, the humidity.
The reason we drink on porches and the labor inequities
we watch like deer in the woods: humidity. In the summer,
the scent of shade by the house. The hostas growing there.
Moss between bricks. A dampness of loam and the lip
of the water table, our yards dipping beneath it. Mosquitoes
singing to their children. Everything at the edge of ponds.
Newt and frog eggs. Our shoes and sticks. My child hallooing
into the depths. His uncle taking him out in the rowboat
without asking, without a life jacket. My brother not a sailor.
We swam that sullen pond once, in desperate summer—rose
steaming, each hair covered in silt, more dirty than before.

Chased from the Illinois
        territory for selling
    snake oil. One dead.

Fleeing on a ship
        from England
    as horse thieves.

Lifting heels from farms
        to join the Confederates.
    Whooping. Hollering.

Every man in my family
        a rebel, known
    to his chickens.

Every woman a
        gardener, baker,
    animal-husbander.

There is little new
        in our furrows,
    on our tongues:

corn and sugar,
        family kindness
    kept in

the family, rows
        of sparkling okra,
    fat in the pan—

you can taste
        the lard in cookies
    and cakes, always—

when you cannot
        see it,
    it is still there,

and when your mother
        says, "too poor
    to own slaves,"

enslavement still
        happened,
    in the house, barn,

in the fields
        and the gardens,
    behind

closed doors until
        the law changed—
    but the letter

of the law is the only
        thing that gave,
    not the spirit.

I've seen the census
        & confession
    in my family's

    scripted, educated
        hands—nothing
    says we were poor

but papers say
　　we did enslave,
　same

as they say we
　　farmed,
　lived

in Louisiana,
　　Arkansas,
　Kentucky.

Same as down
　　by the river,
　moss grows damp

on the trees, algae
　　on rocks
　in the water

and on those rocks
　　a foot can slip
　and slip again.

Keep these failures close,
　　my little love,
　cradle this knowing

like a chick in your
　　hands, shelter its
　feathered bones.

Bennett Place, Durham, North Carolina

A farm home gone green
and light, gone historic,

grown between the doglegged
split-rail fence—known

as *battlefield fence*: easy
to take apart for firewood.

The generals Johnston
and Sherman met each other

here, on the dirt path, asked
the Bennetts for their home

and the Bennetts said yes:
opened their door to surrender

and Citronelle, Alabama;
Galveston, Texas; Doaksville,

Oklahoma followed. Why
is surrender a hard act for us?

We brought the American
chestnut down for our fences

(*worm fence, snake fence*),
let the other fences and walls

also fall now to our fires,
that we might stay warm

together. We are not
talking chickens and foxes.

I said warm not war.
I said surrender.

And in our church last
Sunday: *I surrender all.*

It is dusk / and several men are digging / in a graveyard / small / paper / American flags
the kind teachers keep / on their desks / in a cup / are flying everywhere / the flags litter
the grass / fill the wind / a boy / runs through / the graveyard / his shirt a single Con-
federate flag / now tell me / what / came first: poetry / or the abundance / of the image?
and what / is the reader to do / with abundance in poetry? / *too much* / is a gloss of abun-
dance / and I have been / called that / but when there is too much / of one thing don't
we give / that thing away? / or burn it / in a barrel / as my family did / striking a match
lighting / a paper corner / setting the mess / ablaze / British poets / will tell you how
long / *fire* and *desire* / have rhymed / they will tell you / they did it first / translated the
Italian / the English always / arms and legs / ahead of us / teaching us / of flags and
property / but we made abundance / and too much / our creed / in America / and it
comes for us / in our dreams / narrows to a flag / on a child's body / let us light / this
flag up / to give us a burning / to see by / to make space / for others / to keep / our grave-
yards / unfilled with children / and their parents / to make the white ghosts / of the
South / lonely / deny them our / continued company / our dreamscapes / our poetry

It is arrow after arrow
                in the still-pumping heart

who is the master of art?   (no one)
who wants to master the body of a poem?   (no one should)

   🖎

I have a master in my family tree
Jack Allums
             he will always be there

the male head of a household
a person licensed to command

farmer and enslaver
             sower of seed

his word writ on bodies

   🖎

Even in Amherst   Dickinson's imagination
runs to master

in her third "Master letter," she crosses out the line

     ~~but I knew you had altered me.~~

when Emily crosses a line
she revises   she helms herself

she circumnavigates

          mastery

The mythos of mastery is this—

a canvas sail is said to master   the wind
and a wooden rudder   the sea

but the wind can shred the sail

          and the ocean

dissolve a human tongue

so that it cannot say

       a single word

to make will always be better

         than to master

the field of the page   better

than salt and sugar

      tields

of someone else's labor

IT WAS A FIELD BEFORE IT WAS A BATTLEFIELD

for Luke

It was a green before a fiddler stood on it,
and made mirth, and never stopped playing.
It was grass. Or maybe a greenwood. Maybe
underbrush, thick at your knees. Unparsable.
We have each taken something that belonged
to itself first, something that was once a wide
and open green. What turns red in spring
before it greens? The redbud trees along
the highway, also the human heart. Each
glows lamp-like on the road to church.
Virginia rolls with fields and when I say:
it was a field before it was a battlefield,
you say: "And after." Yes, and after.

Somewhere along the way the word *supper*—meal had as the sun slips down—was lost.
Supper: softer than dinner. Everyone settling like hens in the coop. If there was good-
ness in that house, it was the cornbread on the table and spoonfuls of honey, pats of
butter. The benediction of perfect gravy, rising biscuits. What tenderness was missing
from our speech arrived in the form of corn and beans, tomatoes, blackberry cobbler,
chicken and dumplings. My mother could not say *I love you* for many years, but she
could offer a pecan sweet roll with pink icing, and that was the language of supper.
So much had happened during the day but supper, potentially, mended it. The hens
quieted down in this hour to sleep.

I have not been tender enough,
with the birds on my porch

whose nest I took down, put back,
disturbed. There is more: I looked

at my family tree and wanted
to cut it down. To saw off limbs.

Cut roots that go too deep in the
South. The branches of the US

military. My father's year-long
targeting course at Ft. Leavenworth.

I have put on robes and been
a judge, sat behind the gavel

and in the docks. Sat in the court-
room seats where almost anyone

can sit. I have been all of these
places and persons, all at once.

There is a fable of the body,
where the members want to revolt

against the stomach—but even
a child can see it's all one body.

At last, even the finger, the nail
with its minor crescent, can see.

The chicks with their still-closed eyes.

At night, we do what we are ashamed to do in the day. Under the moon, we send trucks to a campus, a city square—to deserted public places. With the dark as witness, we remove a statue, a plinth. We take pieces away from the picture. The city fountains trickle in the night. The owls hunt. We move quietly among the moths. The trucks growl down the streets with their burdens.

What: the quiet work of words. The doctors
and the nurses fleet as thought. The bindings
and loosenings. The basins with warm, clear
water. The sage and pine of the clean air.
The patient resting, positioned by a window.
In the evening there will be music, a small
glass filled with something warm, the orange
light painterly on a vase of tulips—the red ones
seeming to leap out of the dark. A book lies
nearby, with a marker in it. It is good.
The patient only puts it down to look
at the light. At the light on the tulips.
You can be sick, they think, *and still
the tulips. Still the dark.* The book is light
in their hands. The room is warm. The aim
has always been: do no harm, in this place.
In the place of the book and the tulips.
Even without visitors, the patient feels it.
This place has many rooms. The patient, also.
They put the book, the tulips, the light
inside them. The light has always been
going down. The dark always full of it.

Bitter collards. Rib bones smoking
against our teeth. All the honey
and sugar cannot make it sweet.
This is vinegar's sting—our meat
bites back. Our teeth grind and it
is bone they hit, gristle and ligament.
We leave the dinner table. The leftovers
grow cold. Will there be biscuits
in the morning? Who said there will
be morning? *What is the answer*,
asked Stein on her deathbed.
When Alice said nothing, Stein said:
Then, there is no question, and died.
We wipe the plates tonight. We wash
our hands. Nothing comes clean.
What I thought was an owl
was a dog, barking in the night.

"Having Taken Part in the Late Rebellion" collages language from Jack Allums' Application for Confederate Pardon (1865).

"Poem Ending with a Line from C.D. Wright": the ending line is from C.D. Wright's *Rising, Falling, Hovering* (Copper Canyon Press, 2008).

"Confederate Monuments" has an epigraph from Natasha Trethewey's *Beyond Katrina: A Meditation on the Mississippi Gulf Coast* (University of Georgia Press, 2012).

"Post-Antebellum in the States": the repetitions of "plantation state" are thinking about Brenda Coultas's *The Marvelous Bones of Time* (Coffee House Press, 2007), specifically the lines "Looking from the free state / there is a river then a slave state / Turn around and there is a slave state, a river" (p. 17).

The titles of "Song of the South," "High Cotton," and "Dixie Land Delight" are borrowed/thieved from the Alabama songs of the same names.

"Confederate Statues are Falling This Morning" refers to the toppling of the Confederate Soldiers Monument at the old Durham County Courthouse on August 14, 2017. Seven activists were arrested.

"Regarding the Hooding of the Daughters of the Confederacy Monument" refers to the activism of a citizen of Raleigh, North Carolina.

"Poem Beginning with a Line from Claudia Rankine"—the beginning line is from Claudia Rankine's "Cornel West makes the point..." in *Don't Let Me Be Lonely* (Graywolf Press, 2004).

"This Is the Barbecue We Had Last Night" is language from the back of a lynching postcard of William Stanley, Temple, Texas, 1915, cited in Eula Biss's *Notes from No Man's Land* (Graywolf Press, 2009). Full reverse-side text reads: "This is the barbecue we had last night my picture is to the left with a cross over it your son Joe." The US Postmaster General banned the distribution of lynching postcards in 1908.

ACKNOWLEDGMENTS

The author would like to thank the editors of the following journals, in which these poems appeared, sometimes in previous forms:

About Place Journal, "Poem Ending in a Line from C.D. Wright"
American Poetry Journal, "What Escaped"
Baltimore Review, "Tractors"
Cherry Tree, "The Lives of My Childhood"
EcoTheo Review, "It Was a Field before It Was a Battlefield"
Kenyon Review, "Locusts or Complaint as Protest" and "Poem Beginning with a
     Line from Claudia Rankine"
On the Seawall, "When Someone Says a Poem Is Masterful"
Poems2Go, "Dixie Land Delight"
Southern Humanities Review, "A Visitor Says Things Are Rotting in Durham, NC"
storySouth, "Chicken Farming in the Pelican State"
The McNeese Review, "Confederate Statues Are Falling This Morning" and
     "This Hour"
Thrush Poetry Journal, "The Light Has Always Been Going Down"
UCity Review, "Diving Into the Wreck" (as "Preschool Holiday")

With Thanks

First to my partner Luke, who sustains me. To my children, Beren and Anselm, always up for being read a poem and playing Minecraft: you two are my best poems. To the many strong women in my life. To my teachers, especially Jennifer Atkinson, Eric Pankey, Sally Keith, and Susan Tichy. To Tyree Daye, for his care in reading and shaping this collection. To everyone who has been patient with me. To Ben and Jen (where have you been my whole life?). To the Twitter community who has brought me much joy and companionship in reading, parenting, and teaching. Thanks to Ross White, for his support and trust.

Han VanderHart lives in Durham, North Carolina, under the pines. They have poetry, nonfiction, and reviews published in *Kenyon Review*, *The American Poetry Review*, *Poetry Northwest*, AGNI, *The Adroit Journal*, RHINO Poetry, *Tinderbox Poetry Journal*, *The Rumpus*, *The Chattahoochee Review*, *Southern Humanities Review*, and *The Greensboro Review*. They are the author of the chapbook *Hands Like Birds* (Ethel Press, 2019) and the reviews editor at *EcoTheo Review*.